Complete Preludes, Nocturnes and Waltzes

26 Preludes, 21 Nocturnes, 19 Waltzes for Piano

Frederic Chopin (Composer)

SCHIRMER'S LIBRARY
OF MUSICAL CLASSICS

Vol. 2056

FRÉDÉRIC CHOPIN

Complete Preludes, Nocturnes and Waltzes

For Piano

Edited and fingered by Rafael Joseffy

FRÉDÉRIC FRANÇOIS CHOPIN
(1810–1849)

[or alternately, Fryderyk Franciszek Chopin]

Chopin was a pivotal figure in the history of the piano. He wrote music ideally suited to the "new" instrument that was evolving during his life. As a result of developments in piano technology instruments were capable of producing a broader palate of colors than their predecessors. They also allowed pianists to execute much faster, more intricate, delicate passage-work than earlier instruments. Chopin used these elements of the new pianos, along with the sound-altering capabilities of the *una corda* pedal, to create music full of subtly interwoven melodies and colorful, modal harmonies. He created an expanded role for the piano as a solo instrument, performing his own fluid, expressive music with a delicate touch and tremendous sensitivity. Virtually all of his compositions were either pieces for solo piano or pieces that featured the piano prominently, a unique preoccupation for a composer of the romantic era.

Born near Warsaw, Poland, to a Polish mother and a French father, Chopin was an undeniable prodigy. The boy's precocious playing opened the doors of Warsaw salons, where he quickly became the darling of society. He reveled in the elegance and style of that world. Chopin began writing music as a child, publishing his first pieces at age seven. Following his education at the Warsaw Conservatory, he left Poland for Vienna in 1830 to make a name for himself in a cultural capital. He eventually settled in Paris, where he became a sought-after teacher, and again as a favorite performer in the salons of the wealthy and aristocratic, where educated, cultured people gathered to hear the latest music, poetry, or literature of the day.

Famous for his fussy, fashionable clothing and handsome face, Chopin led a pampered life. A small, frail man weighing just over 100 pounds, he was quite sensitive about his physical stature because he felt it kept him from making a resonant, ample tone on the piano, which he (and his critics) would have liked. Accordingly, Chopin enjoyed playing in the small salons, or drawing rooms. He felt these spaces were suited to his relatively small sound and did not cause him the nervous tension he felt when playing in large halls. In fact, Chopin's legendary reputation as a performer stems from a total of about 30 concert-hall performances over the course of his entire career. Chopin preferred to be known as a composer, a reputation Robert Schumann helped build by famously writing, in review of Chopin's *Variations*, Op. 2, "Hats off, gentlemen, a genius!"

Chopin was never able to return to Poland, due to political upheaval and war there, and he always missed his homeland deeply. He incorporated some of the folk music he heard as a youth into lovely, longing piano pieces. Although he never married, Chopin sustained a nearly decade-long relationship with the bold novelist George Sand (Aurore Dudevant). She lived a wildly bohemian, outspoken lifestyle, smoking cigars and dressing in men's clothing. But she became a tender, maternal care-giver to the composer, creating the happiest, most productive period of his life. Chopin's frail health, diminished by tuberculosis, deteriorated during their years together, plummeting after their break-up. He died two years later, at age 39, and was buried in Paris. Mozart's *Requiem* was performed at his funeral, which was attended by almost 3,000 people.

A prelude in the 19th century is a short piano piece tightly composed on short motifs. The 24 Preludes of Op. 28 are written in every major and minor key, an obvious homage to J.S. Bach. Chopin's Preludes follow a specific sequence of keys in the circle of fifths, with each major key paired with its relative minor. He composed the Preludes as a complete dramatic cycle; however, they are usually performed individually, or in smaller sets. Chopin worked on these Preludes at various times, beginning in 1836, finishing the opus in 1839. They represent a wide spectrum of styles, moods, and technical challenges, and most were, in some capacity, composed as teaching pieces for his students. The Prelude in C-sharp minor, Op. 45, was written when Chopin was at George Sand's summer retreat in Nohant during 1841 and was published in the same year. The Prelude in A-flat major was written during 1834, but remained unpublished until 1918.

A nocturne, as its name implies, evokes dreams and visions of night, capturing a combination of restfulness and restlessness. Chopin's Nocturnes are a perfection of the genre created by John Field during the early years of the 19th century. Chopin was unquestionably inspired in his Nocturnes by the *bel canto* vocal style of Bellini and Donizetti, as was Field before him. Chopin developed the form to new heights of sophistication in these contemplative, often melancholic masterworks through his harmonic and melodic language, while also exploiting the new capabilities of the modern piano as it developed. Like the Preludes, Chopin's Nocturnes were primarily composed for his students, spanning the years 1827 to 1846. They teach a strong sense of right hand *cantabile* playing while the left hand provides the underlying harmonic and rhythmic structure, most commonly in some variation of arpeggio.

Chopin wrote his first Waltz (or Valse in French) in Warsaw at age 17, and continued to write them almost to the end of his life, composing his last in 1848. The composer's history of adopting popular dance forms for his own artistic expressions is well documented not only in the Waltzes, but also in his many Polonaises and Mazurkas. The Waltzes typically fall on extreme ends of the emotional spectrum, from brilliant, exuberant showpieces, to pensive, introspective miniatures. Chopin took the traditional Viennese dance and gave it a distinctly French flavor, perfectly suited to the aristocratic salons in which they were performed.

Rafael Joseffy (1852-1915) was a famous Hungarian-born pianist who settled in New York in 1879. He was a noted Chopin interpreter and teacher, and created the original G. Schirmer editions, collected here, in 1894 and 1915. Joseffy was steeped in the romantic style of the 19th century, and brought that performer's sensibility to the editions. This collection includes seven pieces not edited by Joseffy: the Prelude in A-flat major (1834), the Nocturnes in C-sharp minor (1830) and C minor (1837), and the Waltzes in A-flat major (1827), E-flat major (1830), E-flat major (1840), and A minor (1843). They are presented here free of editorial markings, as a resource for study. The pieces appear at the end of each respective section of this volume.

CONTENTS

PRELUDES

NOCTURNES

WALTZES

à J.C. Kessler

PRELUDE

Frédéric Chopin
Op. 28, No. 1

Agitato

PRELUDE

Frédéric Chopin
Op. 28, No. 2

PRELUDE

Frédéric Chopin
Op. 28, No. 3

*) Carl Tausig, who had a marked preference for a stretchedout position of the fingers, used the following fingering:

PRELUDE

Frédéric Chopin
Op. 28, No. 4

PRELUDE

Frédéric Chopin
Op. 28, No.

Allegro molto

PRELUDE

Frédéric Chopin
Op. 28, No. 6

PRELUDE

Frédéric Chopin
Op. 28, No. 7

Klindworth

PRELUDE

Frédéric Chopin
Op. 28, No. 8

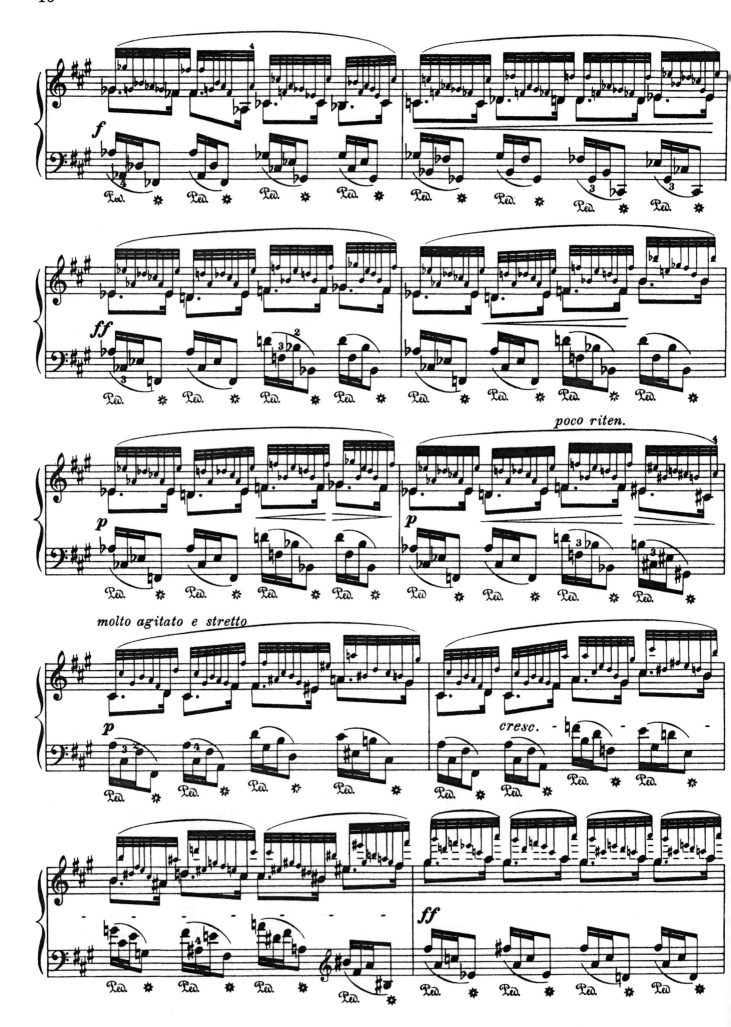

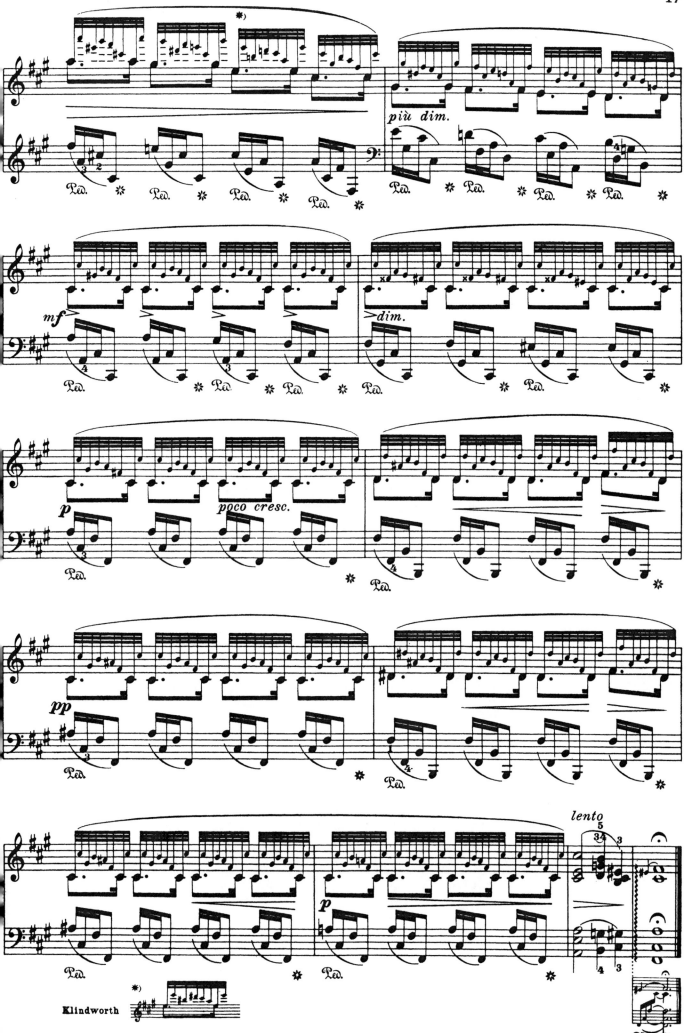

Klindworth

PRELUDE

Frédéric Chopin
Op. 28, No. 9

*) Scholz:

PRELUDE

Frédéric Chopin
Op. 28, No. 10

Allegro molto

PRELUDE

Frédéric Chopin
Op. 28, No. 11

PRELUDE

Frédéric Chopin
Op. 28, No. 12

PRELUDE

Frédéric Chopin
Op. 28, No. 13

PRELUDE

Frédéric Chopin
Op. 28, No. 14

Allegro

PRELUDE

Frédéric Chopin
Op. 28, No. 15

Sostenuto

PRELUDE

Frédéric Chopin
Op. 28, No. 16

Presto con fuoco

Klindworth: *)

or:

PRELUDE

Frédéric Chopin
Op. 28, No. 17

PRELUDE

Frédéric Chopin
Op. 28, No. 18

Klindworth:

PRELUDE

Frédéric Chopin
Op. 28, No. 19

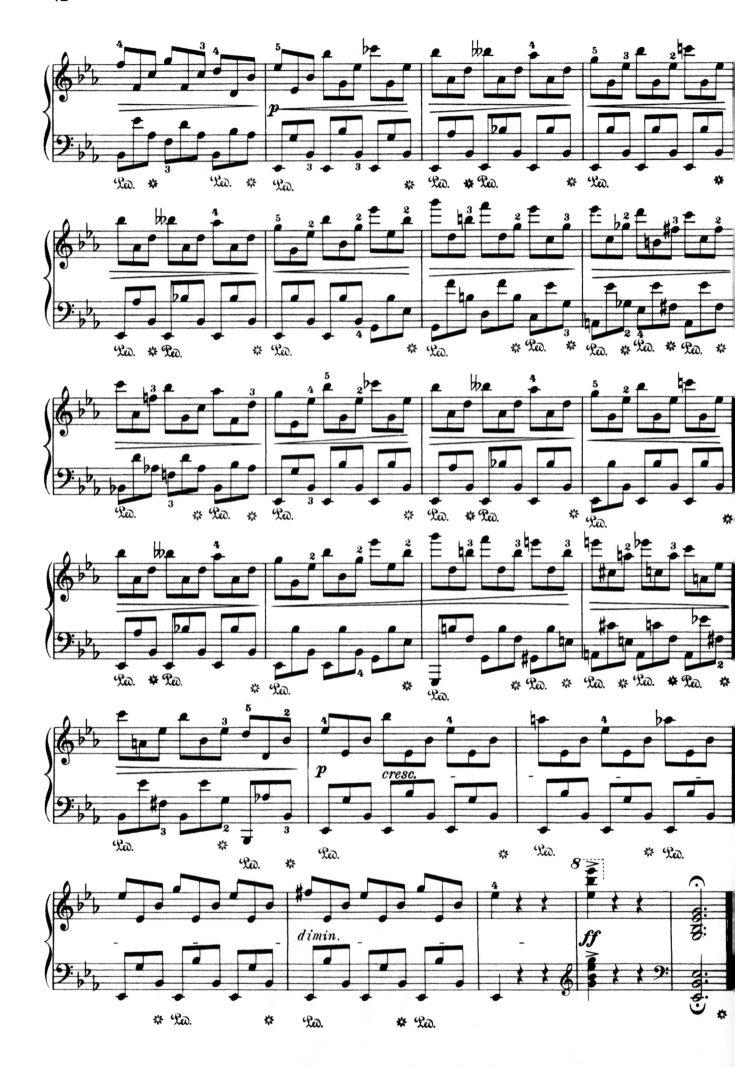

PRELUDE

Frédéric Chopin
Op. 28, No. 20

PRELUDE

Frédéric Chopin
Op. 28, No. 21

PRELUDE

Frédéric Chopin
Op. 28, No. 22

Molto agitato

PRELUDE

Frédéric Chopin
Op. 28, No. 23

Moderato

PRELUDE

Frédéric Chopin
Op. 28, No. 24

Allegro appassionato

à Mademoiselle la Princesse Élisabeth Czernicheff

PRELUDE

Frédéric Chopin
Op. 45

a mon ami Pierre Wolff

PRELUDE

Frédéric Chopin
(1834

Presto con leggierezza

à Madame Camilla Pleyel

NOCTURNE

Frédéric Chopin
Op. 9, No. 1

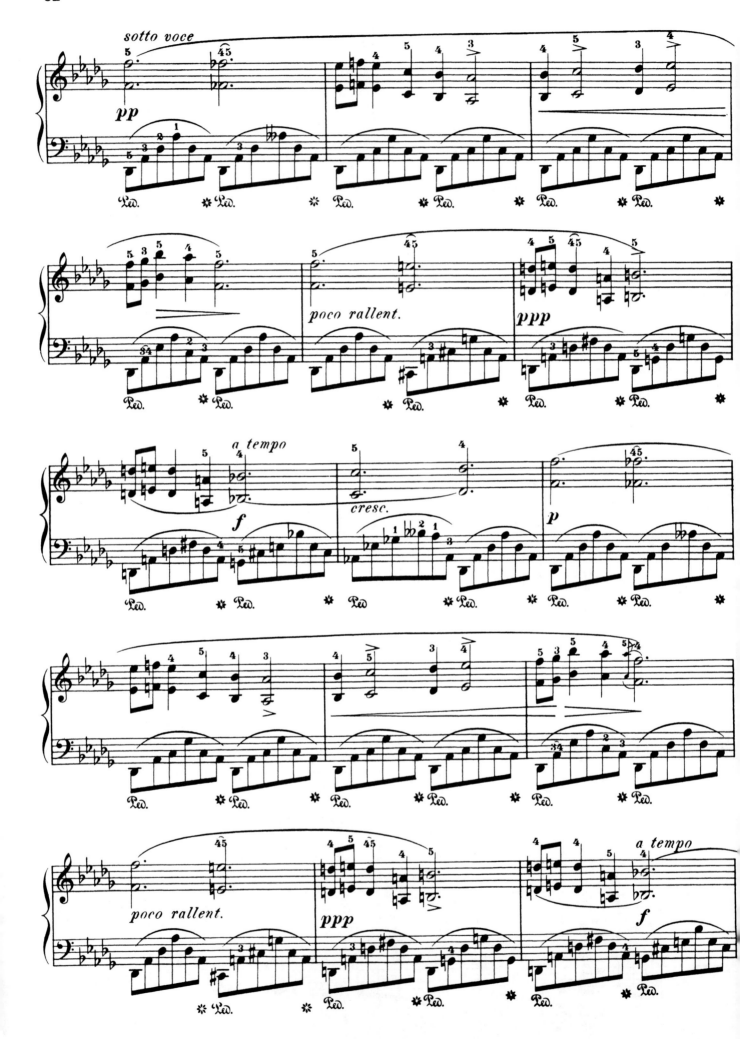

à Madame Camilla Pleyel

NOCTURNE

Frédéric Chopin
Op. 9, No. 2

à Madame Camilla Pleyel

NOCTURNE

Frédéric Chopin
Op. 9, No. 3

à *Mr. Ferdinand Hiller*

NOCTURNE

Frédéric Chopin
Op. 15, No. 1

Andante cantabile (♩ = 69.)

à Mr. Ferdinand Hiller

NOCTURNE

Frédéric Chopin
Op. 15, No. 2

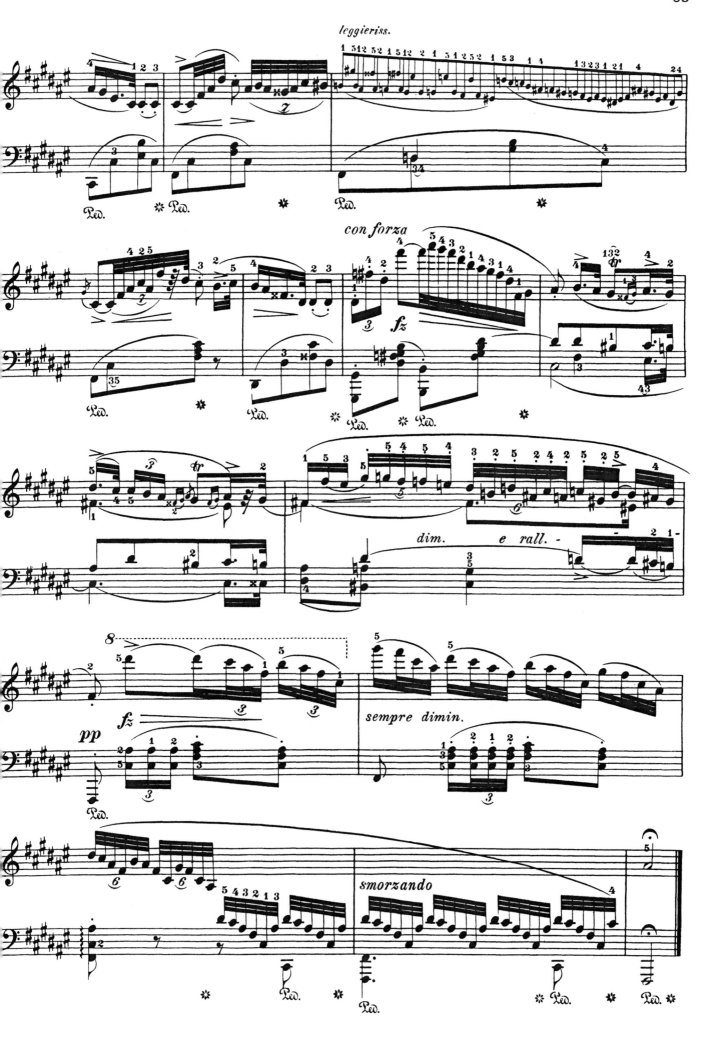

à *Mr. Ferdinand Hiller*

NOCTURNE

Frédéric Chopin
Op. 15, No. 3

à Madame la Comtesse d'Appony

NOCTURNE

Frédéric Chopin
Op. 27, No.

à Madame la Comtesse d'Appony

NOCTURNE

Frédéric Chopin
Op. 27, No. 2

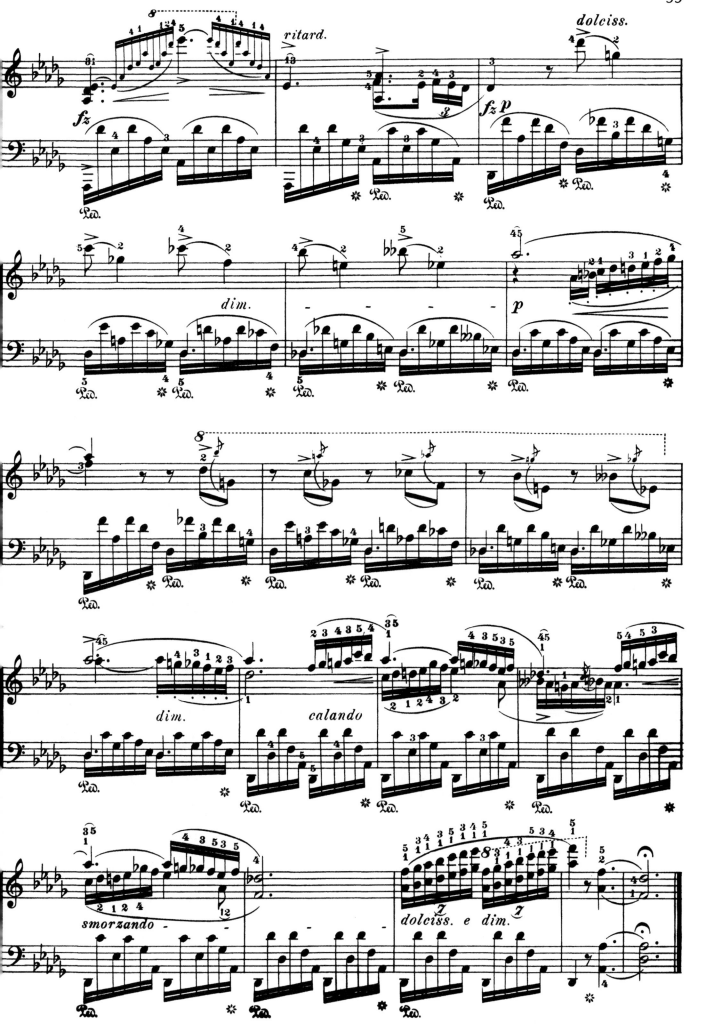

à Madame la Baronne de Billing, née de Courbonne

NOCTURNE

Frédéric Chopin
Op. 32, No. 1

à Madame la Baronne de Billing, née de Courbonne

NOCTURNE

Frédéric Chopin
Op. 32, No. 2

NOCTURNE

Frédéric Chopin
Op. 37, No. 1

NOCTURNE

Frédéric Chopin
Op. 37, No. 2

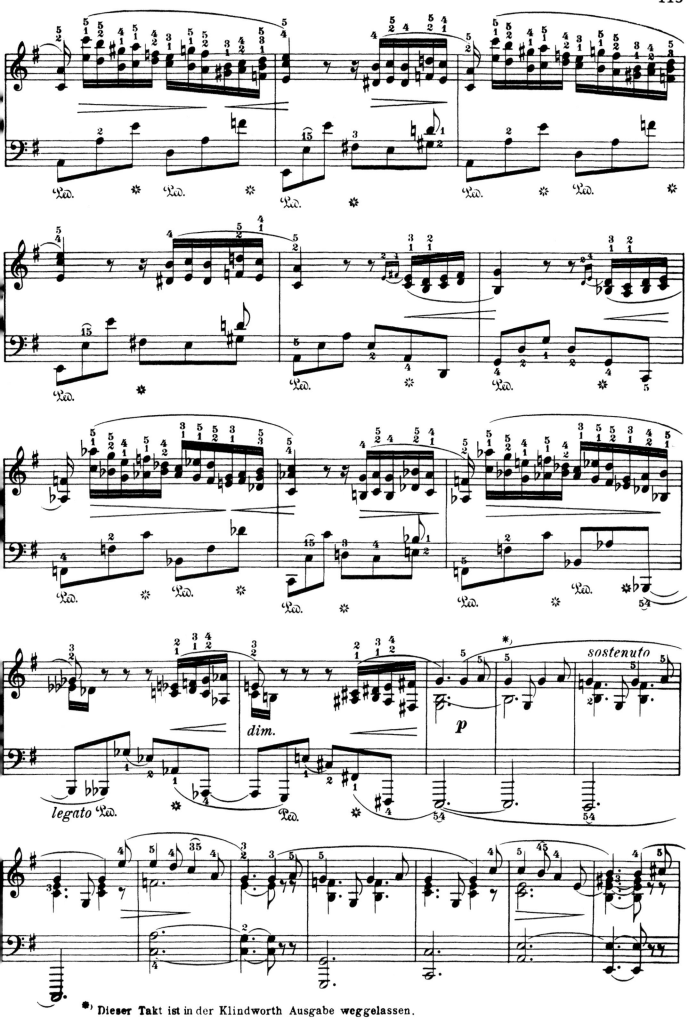

*) Dieser Takt ist in der Klindworth Ausgabe weggelassen.

à Mademoiselle Laura Duperré

NOCTURNE

Frédéric Chopin
Op. 48, No. 1

à Mademoiselle Laura Duperré

NOCTURNE

Frédéric Chopin
Op. 48, No. 2

Andantino

Molto più lento

Klindworth:

à Mademoiselle J.W. Stirling

NOCTURNE

Frédéric Chopin
Op. 55, No. 1

Klindworth:

Scholz:

à Mademoiselle J.W. Stirling

NOCTURNE

Frédéric Chopin
Op. 55, No. 2

Lento sostenuto

à Mademoiselle R. de Könneritz

NOCTURNE

Frédéric Chopin
Op. 62, No.

à Mademoiselle R. de Könneritz

NOCTURNE

Frédéric Chopin
Op. 62, No. 2

Lento
sostenuto

NOCTURNE

Frédéric Chopin
Op. 72, No. 1

NOCTURNE

Frédéric Chopin
(1830)

Lento con gran espressione

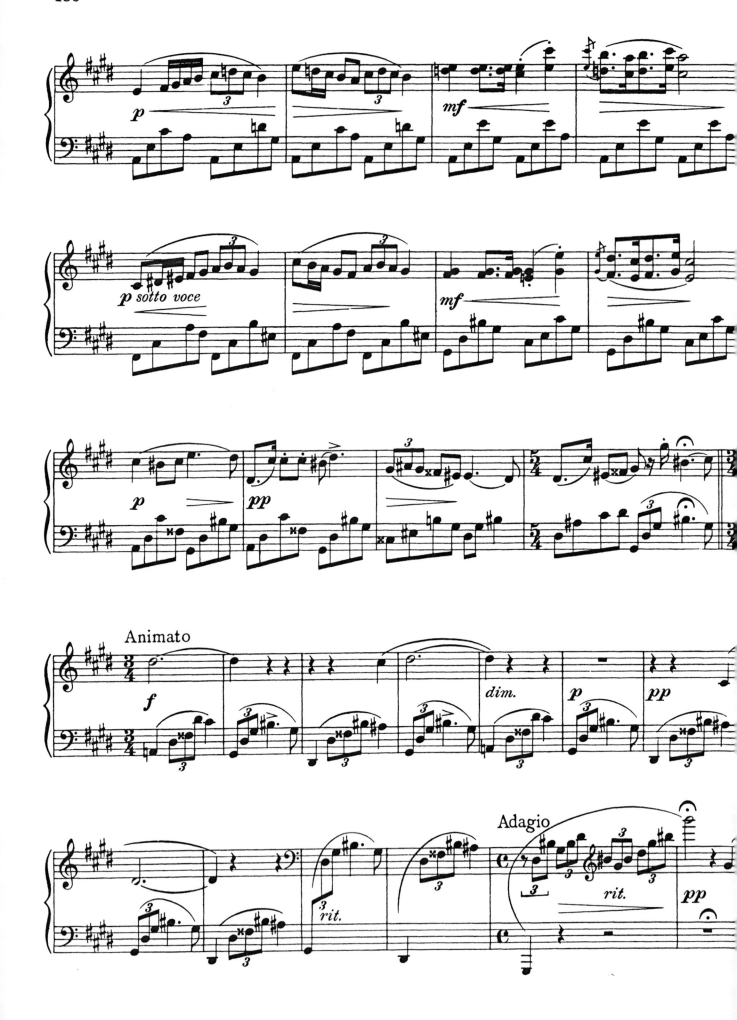

Tempo I

NOCTURNE

Frédéric Chopin
(1837)

Andante sostenuto

à Laura Harsford

GRAND VALSE BRILLANTE

Frédéric Chopin
Op. 18

à Mademoiselle de Thun Hohenstein

VALSE BRILLANTE

Frédéric Chopin
Op. 34, No.

à Madame G. d'Ivry

VALSE BRILLANTE

Frédéric Chopin
Op. 34, No. 2

à Mademoiselle A. d'Eichthal

VALSE BRILLANTE

Frédéric Chopin
Op. 34, No. 3

WALTZ

Frédéric Chopin
Op. 42

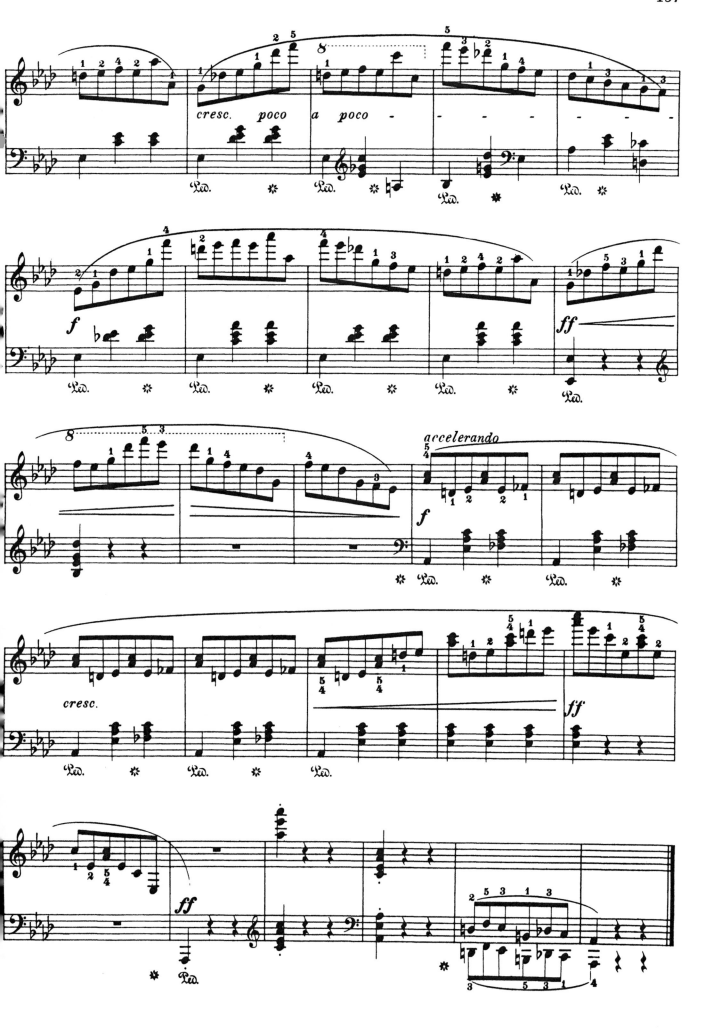

à Madame la Comtesse Delphine Potocka

WALTZ

Frédéric Chopin
Op. 64, No. 1

Molto vivace

à Madame Nathaniel de Rothschild

WALTZ

Frédéric Chopin
Op. 64, No.

Klindworth:

à la Comtesse Katharina Bronicka

WALTZ

Frédéric Chopin
Op. 64, No. 3

Moderato

poco a poco accel. al fine

WALTZ

Frédéric Chopin
Op. 69, No. 1

WALTZ

Frédéric Chopin
Op. 69, No. 2

WALTZ

Frédéric Chopin
Op. 70, No. 1

WALTZ

Frédéric Chopin
Op. 70, No. 2

WALTZ

Frédéric Chopin
Op. 70, No. 3

WALTZ

Frédéric Chopin
Op. Posthumous

WALTZ

Frédéric Chopin
Op. Posthumous

Tempo di Valse

Ped. simile

WALTZ

Frédéric Chopin
(1827

Trio

D.C. al Fine

WALTZ

Frédéric Chopin
(1830

WALTZ

Frédéric Chopin
(1840)

Sostenuto

WALTZ

Frédéric Chopin
(1843

CPSIA information can be obtained at www.ICGtesting.com
Printed in the USA
LVOW022041091011

249769LV00001B/1/P